☑ W9-BLN-682

IN THEIR OWN WORDS

THE WRIGHT BROTHERS

George Sullivan

SCHOLASTIC
REFERENCE

Copyright © 2002 by George Sullivan

All rights reserved. Published by Scholastic Inc.

SCHOLASTIC and associated logos are trademarks and/or registered trademarks of Scholastic Inc.

No part of this publication may be reproduced, or stored in a retrieval system, or transmitted in any form or by any means, electronic, mechanical, photocopying, recording, or otherwise, without written permission of the publisher. For information regarding permission, write to Scholastic Inc., Attention: Permissions Department, 555 Broadway, New York, NY 10012.

LIBRARY OF CONGRESS CATALOGING-IN-PUBLICATION DATA

Sullivan, George, 1927–
The Wright brothers/George Sullivan
p.   cm.—(In their own words)
Includes bibliographical references and index.
Summary: A biography of the brothers responsible for developing the first airplane, featuring excerpts from their journal entries, letters, and drawings.
1. Wright, Orville, 1871–1948—Juvenile literature.   2. Wright, Wilbur, 1867–1912—Juvenile literature.   3. Aeronautics—United States—Biography—Juvenile literature.
4. Inventors—United States—Biography—Juvenile literature.   5. Aeronautics—United States—History—Juvenile literature.   [1. Wright, Orville, 1871–1948.
2. Wright, Wilbur, 1867–1912.   3. Aeronautics—Biography.]   I. Title.   II. In their own words (Scholastic)
TL540.W7 S84 2002
629.13'092'2—dc21
[B]   2001034477

ISBN 0-439-26320-4

10 9 8 7   03 04 05 06

Composition by Brad Walrod
Printed in the U.S.A.
First printing, March 2002

CONTENTS

INTRODUCTION

"WE GAVE [THE] MACHINE [ITS] first test today....The machinery all worked in an entirely satisfactory manner and seems reliable....There is now no question of our final success...."

These are the words of Wilbur Wright. They are from a letter he wrote on December 14, 1903, to his sister, Katharine, and their father, Bishop Milton Wright.

Wilbur wrote from a remote, windswept North Carolina beach not far from Kitty Hawk, a tiny fishing village. Three days after that letter was written, on December 17, 1903, Wilbur and his brother Orville made history. With Orville at the controls, they flew their frail-looking aircraft for the first time.

The flight lasted only twelve seconds. It covered 120 feet. Many Little League players can throw a baseball that far.

That flight was very special, though. It marked the first time a flying machine that could be controlled in the air had left the ground under its own power. It was the first time a human had actually flown.

The Wright brothers were an odd-looking pair as they busied themselves on that lonely North Carolina beach. They wore suits and shirts with starched collars and neckties. A handful of local people watched them.

Back home in Dayton, Ohio, the Wright brothers ran a bicycle shop. They liked to tinker. They built not only bicycles but also toys and a newspaper printing press. In 1896, they became interested in human flight.

They read everything they could on the subject. They began experimenting with kites.

In 1909, Orville (left) and Wilbur Wright posed for this photograph on the porch of their Dayton, Ohio, home. They were already world famous.

Using wood, wire, and lightweight fabric, the brothers built a series of gliders. They tested these airplanes without motors on a sandy stretch of North Carolina's Outer Banks.

Piloting their gliders paid off. The Wrights learned how to control an aircraft. They became masters of the air.

At the time they flew the first powered aircraft, Wilbur was thirty-six years old and Orville was thirty-two.

Wilbur was quiet and intense. He was more energetic than his younger brother. In school, he was the better student. He had a drive to succeed.

Wilbur was sure of himself. Wilbur "is never rattled in his thought or temper," his father once said of him.

Orville was the more talkative of the two. He was friendlier. He always saw the brighter side of things. He was the more spirited of the two boys. He was, as his father described him, "excitable." He liked practical jokes.

Hundreds of books have been written about the

Wright brothers and their remarkable flying machine. Thousands of articles about them have appeared in newspapers and magazines.

Much of what we know about the Wrights and their work comes from the brothers themselves. They both kept diaries. They filled notebooks with comments and drawings.

The Wrights also wrote lots of letters. They wrote several hundred letters to Octave Chanute, a pioneer in the study of early aircraft. In these, they often described how their work was progressing.

From their letters, diaries, and notebooks, we can discover how the Wright brothers lived and worked. We can come to understand how they solved the mysteries of flight.

These personal papers of the Wright brothers are called primary sources. In seeking to learn about a person or the past, historians use both primary sources and secondary sources. Primary sources are actual records that have been handed down from the past.

Letters, diaries, and notebooks aren't the only

by noon and got the
machine out on the
tracks in front of the
building ready for a
trial from the level.
The wind was gradually
dying and by the time
we were ready was blow-
ing only about 4 to 5
meters per. sec. After
waiting several hours
to see whether it would
breeze up again we took
the machine in.

Thursday, Dec. 17th

When we got up a
wind of between 20 and
25 miles was blowing from
the north. We got the
machine out early and
put out the signal to the
men at the station. Before
we were quite ready, John
T. Daniels, W. S. Dough,
A. D. Etheridge, W. C.
Brinkley of Manteo, and
Johnny Moore, of Nags
Head arrived. After

running the engine and
propellers a few min-
utes to get them in working
order, I got on the machine
at 10:35 for the first
trial. The wind according
to our anemometers at
this time was blowing a
little over 20 miles (cor-
rected) 27 miles accord-
ing to the government an-
emometer at Kitty Hawk.
On slipping the rope
the machine started off
increasing in speed to
probably 7 or 8 miles. The
machine lifted from the
truck just as it was
entering on the fourth rail.
Mr. Daniels took a pic-
ture just as it left the
tracks. I found the
control of the front rud-
der quite difficult on
account of its being bal-
anced too near the center
and thus had a tendency
to turn itself when started
so that the rudder was
turned too far on one
side and then too

Orville's diary entry for December 17, 1903, describes the brothers' first
manned flight in a heavier-than-air machine.

primary sources. Newspapers and magazines that date to the time of the Wrights are primary sources, too. So are census records and tax records.

You and your family have your own primary sources. A birth certificate, a marriage license, and a driver's license are primary sources. So are report cards, high school yearbooks, and job application forms.

A secondary source is a secondhand source. It is a description of an event by someone who did not witness it.

A history textbook is a secondary source. So are encyclopedias such as the *World Book*. Recently written books or magazine articles about the Wright brothers are secondary sources, too.

Primary sources can be revealing. For example, Orville and Wilbur Wright are usually looked upon as equals in solving the technical problems of flight. Their success was a shared experience, say most textbooks.

But a careful reading of primary sources can lead to a different judgment. When he first became interested in the problems of human flight, Wilbur often wrote to his father. In these letters, it is clear that Orville was not involved. Wilbur speaks of "my plans" and "my observations." He refers to "my experiments" and "my machine." It is never "we" or "our."

These letters are important pieces of evidence. They have led some historians to conclude that Wilbur played the leading role in overcoming the problems the brothers faced. He showed the way. His kid brother Orville, at least at the beginning, merely helped.

Wilbur, of course, did come to realize that he could not find the solutions to the problems of human flight by himself. "The problem is too great for one man...," he wrote. Teamwork was vital to the success of the Wright brothers.

This book is a secondary source. But it makes use of many primary sources. It draws upon the letters, diaries, and notebooks of the Wrights, repeating their own words. In so doing, it seeks to tell the real story of the Wright brothers and their great success.

THE BROTHERS

WILBUR AND ORVILLE WRIGHT were brought up in a warm and loving Midwestern family. There were five children: four boys and one girl.

Wilbur once wrote of Orville and the brothers' attachment for each other. "From the time we were little children," said Wilbur, "my brother Orville and myself lived together, played together, worked together and, in fact, thought together. Nearly everything that was done in our lives has been the result of conversations, suggestions, and discussions between us."

Wilbur was the third son of Milton Wright and his wife, Susan. He was born on a small farm near Millville, Indiana, on April 16, 1867. Wilbur's older brothers were Lorin and Reuchlin, nicknamed Roosh.

Orville was born four years after Wilbur, on August 19, 1871, in Dayton, Ohio. The Wrights' one daughter, Katharine, the youngest member of the family, was born in 1874. Like Orville, she was born in Dayton.

A special closeness developed among Wilbur, Orville, and their sister, Katharine. It would last all of their lives.

The children's parents had first met at Hartsville College in Indiana. Susan was a student there. Milton was an instructor. They married on Thanksgiving Day, 1859.

Besides being a teacher, Milton Wright was also a minister. He later became a bishop in the United Brethren Church of Christ. His work required that the family move often.

The Wrights settled in Dayton, Ohio, in 1869. They later lived in Cedar Rapids, Iowa, and Richmond, Indiana, before returning to Dayton in 1884. Orville and Wilbur were to live most of their

Susan Wright, Orville and Wilbur's mother, and Bishop Milton Wright, the brothers' father.

lives in a seven-room house their parents owned at 7 Hawthorn Street in Dayton.

The Wright family was unusual for the time in that both parents had gone to college. Although there were a good number of colleges for men in the 1850s, there were few for women. Susan Wright studied literature at Hartsville College.

The Wright home was filled with books. The children were urged to read at an early age. They were also encouraged to be curious, to find things out.

Bishop Wright believed that toys should not be mere playthings. Toys should help children to learn.

One day when Orville was seven and Wilbur was eleven, Bishop Wright came home with an unusual present. It was a small helicopter toy made of paper, cork, and light wood.

The bishop turned the toy's four-bladed propeller, which twisted two rubber bands. He tossed the helicopter, its propeller spinning, toward the boys. The toy rose to the ceiling.

The boys were awed by the gift. They called it "the bat."

Many years later, Orville said that the small toy had triggered the boys' interest in the art of flying. "We built a number of copies of this toy, which flew successfully," Orville wrote. "But when we undertook to fly the toy on a much larger scale, it failed to work so well.

"The reason for this was not understood by us at the time," Orville added, "so we finally abandoned the experiments."

Orville, as a nine-year-old, told of an early

The Wright brothers in 1879; Wilbur (left) was 12, Orville 8.

experiment in a postcard to his father. The experiment involved a can with a long spout through which oil or other liquids could be poured.

"The other day I took a machine can and filled it with water," Orville wrote, "and then I put it on the stove. I waited a while and the [boiling] water came squirting out the top by a foot...."

Both Wilbur and Orville went to public schools. They were good students.

From an early age, both boys were comfortable

with tools. They liked to make things. Orville built and sold kites. When Bishop Wright put out a small newspaper, Wilbur constructed a special machine that folded the papers for mailing.

In high school, the boys built a series of printing presses. One of the presses could print 1,000 pages an hour, even though it was homemade.

The Wright family had its share of troubles. Their mother, Susan Wright, suffered from tuberculosis, a disease of the lungs. Her condition kept getting worse. By the time the family moved to Dayton, she needed constant care.

Bad luck also struck Wilbur. When he was nineteen and playing on a high school ice hockey team, he was hit in the face with a wild swing of a hockey stick. Wilbur was badly cut around his mouth. He lost several front teeth.

The accident changed his life. He dropped out of school and seldom left the house. Wilbur's goal had been to go to college and become a minister. He gave up those plans.

His brother Reuchlin was now married and living

The Wrights' family home once occupied a narrow lot on Hawthorn Street in Dayton, Ohio. In 1936, Henry Ford had the home moved to Greenfield Village in Dearborn, Michigan, its present location, where it is pictured.

away from home. Lorin also had left home. Katharine and Orville were at school.

Wilbur spent much of his time reading. He also served as his mother's nurse, caring for her every need. "Such devotion had rarely been equaled...," Milton Wright said.

Susan Wright died in 1889. Afterward, Wilbur continued to live at home.

Meanwhile, eighteen-year-old Orville was more

interested in his printing presses than his education. He quit school and went into the printing business. He hired Ed Sines, a close friend, as an assistant.

As one of his first ventures, Orville published a neighborhood newspaper. He called it the *West Side News*. Orville was listed as the publisher of the weekly paper. Wilbur became the editor.

After a year, the brothers changed the newspaper from a weekly to a daily. They renamed it the *Evening Item*. The brothers worked hard to make the *Item* a success. But they were no match for Dayton's big papers. After three months, the *Item* went out of business.

The brothers then focused on other kinds of printing work. They began producing business cards, personalized stationery, posters, and advertising circulars for local merchants.

They also printed a four-page weekly newspaper for the African-American community of Dayton. Called *The Tattler*, the paper was written by Paul Dunbar, a school friend of Orville's. Dunbar was the son of escaped slaves. He was the only African-American student in Dayton's Central High School.

Dunbar held Orville in high regard. On a wall in the brothers' print shop, he scribbled this verse:

> *Orville Wright is out of sight*
> *In the printing business.*
> *No other mind is half as bright*
> *As his'n is.*

The Tattler lasted only a few weeks. In later years, Paul Dunbar became a notable poet and novelist.

By the early 1890s, the Wright brothers had entered their twenties. They began to lose interest in the printing business. They had found another interest. It would keep them busy for several years.

BICYCLE MADNESS

A POPULAR CRAZE SWEPT THE NATION during the early 1890s. Americans fell in love with the "safety bicycle."

Up until that time, the only bicycles in use had huge front wheels. The rider was seated high in the air, four or five feet above the ground. Keeping balanced was a real challenge.

The safety bicycle was different. Its front and rear wheels were both the same size. They were much smaller than those of earlier bicycles. If a rider lost his or her balance, there was much less distance to fall.

The new bicycles had air-filled tires and sturdy frames. They also had coaster brakes, the type of brakes operated by putting reverse pressure on the pedals. In 1896, the *Atlantic Monthly* called the safety bicycle "one of the world's great inventions."

Both women and men became eager cyclists. (The automobile was not yet in wide use.) Manufacturers turned out bicycles by the millions.

Orville and Wilbur got caught up in the mania. To Wilbur, cycling meant long rides in the country. Orville enjoyed track racing. He won at least three races.

When their bikes broke down, Orville and Wilbur made the repairs themselves. They got so good at it that their friends began bringing their bikes to them when they needed fixing.

Late in 1892, the brothers opened a small storefront shop where they repaired bicycles. They also began renting and selling bikes. Orville's friend Ed Sines was put in charge of the printing business.

The bicycle business soon became more successful than the printing operation. Moving to larger quarters, the brothers began doing business as the Wright Cycle Company.

Business was always good during the spring and

summer. But with the arrival of winter and its cold weather, interest in cycling waned.

Orville and Wilbur found plenty to do with their free time during the winter months. They built spacious front and side porches for the family home on Hawthorn Street. They made shutters for all the windows.

The two brothers also developed an interest in photography. In a shed behind the house, they set up a darkroom. There they developed their negatives and made their own photographic prints.

To increase profits at the Wright Cycle Company, they decided to produce their own brand of bicycles. They bought tubing, spokes, chains, pedals, handlebars, and other parts from different factories. Then they put them together.

The Wright Cycle Company later moved into one half of a two-story brick building at 1127 West Third Street in Dayton. At the rear of the building there was a good-sized space for a workshop.

Meanwhile, their sister, Katharine, had graduated from high school. She began attending Oberlin

The Wright brothers' bicycle shop on West Third Street in Dayton. This photograph depicts the building after it was purchased by Henry Ford and moved to Greenfield Village in Dearborn, Michigan.

College in Oberlin, Ohio, not far from Cleveland. Bishop Wright continued to tend to church matters and was frequently away. Orville and Wilbur were home alone most of the time.

One day late in the summer of 1896, Wilbur read a news story that jolted him. Otto Lilienthal had died.

Wilbur knew that name well. Otto Lilienthal, a

Otto Lilienthal inspired the Wright brothers with his glider experiments. Above, Lilienthal test-flies a double-wing glider.

German man, was a pioneer in the design of gliders. Gliders were aircraft without engines. Lilienthal had become famous for making flights while hanging from a glider that had batlike wings. He would strap the wings to his back, then launch himself into the wind from the top of a small hill. When the wind was strong, he was able to soar for as long as fifteen seconds.

In a five-year period beginning in 1891, Lilienthal

made more than 2,000 short flights. *McClure's Magazine* called Lilienthal "The Flying Man."

Lilienthal's final flight took place on the afternoon of August 9, 1896, a Sunday. He had reached a height of about fifty feet when a sudden gust pitched the forward edge of the wings upward. The glider then lurched to the right. Lilienthal thrashed about in an effort to gain control, but he could not.

The glider plunged to the ground, breaking Lilienthal's spine. He died the next day in a hospital in Berlin, Germany.

Lilienthal's tragic death was reported in American newspapers. He was described as someone who had given up his life for science. He was looked upon as a hero.

For Wilbur, Lilienthal's death was a turning point. He would later write that his "own active interest" in problems having to do with the design and use of aircraft "dates back to the death of Lilienthal in 1896." Both he and Orville began to read whatever they could find on the subject of flight.

Wilbur expressed a "growing belief" that man could learn to fly. Insects and birds with many different types of bodies "were flying every day," Wilbur had noted. It "was reasonable to suppose," he said, "that man might also fly."

In the spring of 1899, Wilbur wrote to the Smithsonian Institution in Washington, D.C., for information about human flight. To be sure that his letter would be taken seriously, Wilbur declared, "I am an enthusiast, but not a crank in the sense that I have some pet theories as to the proper construction of a flying machine. I wish to avail myself [make use] of all that is already known. . . ."

The Smithsonian sent Wilbur four pamphlets, some reprints of articles, and a list of books. Within a matter of months, the brothers were at work building their own experimental aircraft. Their bicycle business began to fade in importance.

A MATTER
OF CONTROL

FOR WHAT ARE THE WRIGHT BROTHERS known? Inventing the airplane is what most people say.

That isn't completely correct.

From the beginning, the Wrights sought to do what no one else had done. They wanted to design and build a flying machine that could do more than go up and go down.

They wanted to be able to control an aircraft in the sky. That was their chief goal.

Control meant being able to tilt the wings to the right or left when turning the aircraft. Control also meant keeping the aircraft balanced.

Flying, the brothers understood, was something

like bicycle riding. Unless the cyclist kept balanced, the bicycle toppled over. It was the same with a flying machine. If balance wasn't maintained, the machine could fall from the sky.

The brothers began their study of human flight in the spring of 1899. They became familiar with studies conducted by Professor Samuel Langley, a noted scientist and secretary of the Smithsonian Institution. Langley's experiments had dealt with powered flight.

Langley and his staff built more than 100 aircraft models. They flew them around an indoor track. In his early experiments, Langley's models were powered by rubber bands. His later designs had small steam engines. Langley called his model aircraft aerodromes.

In the spring of 1896, Langley moved his experiments outdoors. At the time, his aerodromes featured two fragile wings, one behind the other. Each model weighed twenty-six pounds.

Langley loaded two of the models onto an old houseboat and carried them out into the Potomac

River near Quantico, Virginia. His plan was to launch the aircraft from atop the houseboat's roof. A spring-powered catapult would hurl the models into the air.

On the afternoon of May 6, 1896, Langley was ready. As the first of the models was launched, a wire that held the two wings in place snapped. The aerodrome veered to the right and plunged into the water.

Samuel Langley pioneered in the design and construction of heavier-than-air flying machines.

Another aerodrome—known as aerodrome No. 5 —was lifted into place. An assistant pulled a lever. The catapult fired, sending the miniature airplane rushing down a track and into the air. It dipped slightly, then caught the wind and began climbing. Langley and his crew watched in awe.

The tiny aircraft remained airborne for ninety seconds. Then its fuel gave out. Aerodrome No. 5 glided to a landing on the water.

The aircraft had traveled about 3,000 feet through the air. It had reached a speed of twenty-five miles an hour.

Langley was overjoyed. And it was no wonder. Aerodrome No. 5 had completed the first successful flight of an aircraft powered by an engine.

But Langley had not solved some critical problems. His model aircraft had taken off. It had landed. But there had been no attempt to control it. No one could rotate the wings to the right or left in making a turn. No one could keep an aircraft balanced in the sky.

The problem of control was on their minds when the Wrights watched buzzards soar in the sky. These graceful birds circled and kept themselves balanced by tilting and twisting their wings.

When a bird wanted to adjust its flight, it tilted one wing up, the opposite wing down. The bird would then roll its body toward the lowered wing. The result was a gentle turn.

Orville was sure an airplane could be developed that would imitate these twisting movements. As he later wrote, "We could not understand that there was anything about a bird that could not be built on a larger scale and used by man."

But no one had yet figured out how to tilt or twist a plane's wings like that of a bird. The wings of Lilienthal's gliders did not bend, nor did the wings of Langley's aircraft models.

How could an aircraft's wings be tilted and twisted like those of a bird? That was the question the Wright brothers sought to answer.

One summer evening when he was tending the bicycle shop by himself, Wilbur hit upon the answer. A customer came in to buy a bicycle inner tube. Wilbur removed the tube from its long, narrow cardboard box. While talking with the customer, he happened to twist the ends of the box in opposite directions.

He suddenly realized that an aircraft's wings could be twisted in a similar fashion. The twisting would cause one wing to tilt up, the other down. The result would be a graceful turn.

After he closed the shop that night, Wilbur took the box home and showed Orville his discovery. The brothers then decided to build and test a glider that included the paper-box principle. "We began construction of a model...within a day or two," Orville later wrote.

In the workroom of the bicycle shop, the Wrights built their glider out of split bamboo, paper, and string. Designed to be flown as a kite, the model took the form of a biplane. A biplane has two wings, one above the other. Each of the model's wings was five feet in length.

Wilbur would be able to control the model with a stick he held in each hand. Cords ran from the sticks to the model's wingtips. By tilting the sticks in one direction or another, Wilbur could twist the model's wings in opposite directions.

Late in July, Wilbur took the model to a field

where he and Orville had once flown kites. When he had the model up in the air, Wilbur began working the control sticks. He felt a rush of excitement as he made the model respond to his commands to climb, dive, or circle to the right or left.

Sometimes the model was unruly. The wings would tilt abruptly in one direction or another. But Wilbur was able to adjust the angle of the wings and return the model to level flight. He was able to keep the model balanced.

Some neighborhood children stopped to watch. At one point, Wilbur put the model into a steep

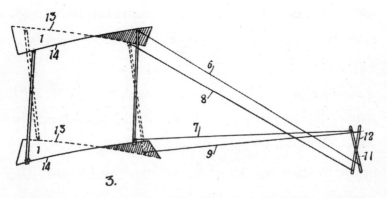

The Wright brothers' sketch of their experimental kite. By warping the wings, they could make the kite turn.

dive. It swooped down toward where the children were standing. They had to throw themselves to the ground to avoid being hit.

The test convinced the Wrights that they were on the right track. They were ready to take the next step. They were ready to begin experiments with what Orville called "a man-carrying machine."

CHAPTER 5

TO KITTY HAWK

THE WRIGHT BROTHERS' PLANS TO build and test-fly a man-carrying glider had to wait. Through the spring and into the summer of 1900, their bicycle business kept them busy.

Wilbur did find time, however, to pick a test site. He wanted a place where there were enough strong and steady winds to be able to lift the glider into the air.

Wilbur decided to write to Octave Chanute for advice. Like Otto Lilienthal and Samuel Langley, Chanute was an expert on the problems of flight.

Born in Paris, Chanute had been brought to the United States as a boy of six. After attending private schools, Chanute excelled as an engineer who built bridges, roads, and dams.

Once he became interested in human flight, Chanute became a leader in the field. He wrote articles about aviation. His book, *Problems in Flying Machines*, was well known to Wilbur.

Wilbur wrote to Chanute for the first time on May 13, 1900. From that date, Chanute became one of the brothers' closest friends and most eager supporters.

Wilbur described himself to the sixty-eight-year-old Chanute as a young fellow who held "the belief that flight is possible to man." Wilbur was fearful of where his belief might lead him. He said he was afraid that it "will soon cost me an increased amount of money, if not my life."

Chanute suggested locations in California and Florida where the Wrights could test their glider. While both sites had better-than-average winds, neither had a long, wide, sandy beach. Besides wind, Wilbur wanted a soft landing place.

Wilbur then wrote to the U.S. Weather Bureau

in Washington, D.C., for advice. A North Carolina fishing village named Kitty Hawk was among the sites the Weather Bureau mentioned. Kitty Hawk was a small settlement on the Outer Banks, a long string of sand-covered islands off the North Carolina coast. Besides nearly constant winds, Kitty Hawk had

Octave Chanute, a noted American civil engineer and aviation enthusiast, aided and encouraged the Wrights' experiments.

a wide, sandy beach that stretched for miles.

Bill Tate, the postmaster in Kitty Hawk, learned of Wilbur's interest. He wrote to him and encouraged him. "This in my opinion would be a fine place," Tate said. "Our winds are always steady, generally 10 to 20 miles...per hour."

Tate also promised to help. "If you decide to try your machine here & come," he wrote, "I will take pleasure in doing all I can for your convenience & success & pleasure...."

Kitty Hawk sounded perfect. The brothers decided that they would take a vacation from their bicycle shop later that summer. Business would be slower then. They would travel to Kitty Hawk and test their glider there.

By the time Wilbur received Bill Tate's letter, the glider was almost finished. It was a biplane with a lightweight wood frame. Its seventeen-foot wings were covered in a tightly woven cotton cloth. The aircraft weighed about fifty pounds.

The pilot would lie face down on the lower wing. From this position, he would control the rectangle-shaped panel called the elevator. (In most modern airplanes, the elevator is part of the tail.) By tilting the elevator up or down, he could make the glider nose up or nose down.

The pilot's feet rested on a metal bar. The bar was linked by wires to the wings. By pressing on the bar with one foot or the other, the pilot could twist the wings in opposite directions. When one wing twisted up, the other twisted down.

For example, if the right wing were twisted up and the left wing down, the plane would turn to the left. This system also kept the aircraft balanced.

Before packing up the glider parts and shipping them to Kitty Hawk, Wilbur wrote to his father. He said, "I am intending to start in a few days for a trip to the coast of North Carolina...for the purpose of making some experiments with a flying machine.

"It is my belief that flight is possible," he continued, "and...I think there is a slight possibility of achieving fame and fortune from it."

Wilbur left for Kitty Hawk soon after. It was a difficult journey, taking seven days. There was no bridge yet connecting the Outer Banks with the North Carolina mainland. Wilbur had to hire a boat to get there.

In 1900, the village of Kitty Hawk was made up of a handful of weather-beaten wood-frame homes.

They were scattered among the long-leafed pines and tall oaks that lined the sound.

To the east, near the beach, was a U.S. lifesaving station with a boathouse and lookout tower. It was one of seven lifesaving stations on the Outer Banks. On stormy nights, crew members of the lifesaving stations patrolled the beaches. They carried lanterns or signal flares to warn ships away from danger points.

At first, Wilbur roomed with the Tate family. When a freight boat delivered the crates containing the glider parts, he began putting the aircraft together.

"I have my machine nearly finished," he said in a letter to his father that is dated September 23, 1900.

He sought to assure his father that there was nothing to worry about. "In my experiments I do not expect to rise many feet from the ground," he said, and added, "I do not intend to take dangerous chances...."

1900

WILBUR HAD BEEN AT KITTY HAWK for about a week and a half when Orville arrived. Orville stayed in Wilbur's room at the Tates' house for a few days. Then the brothers set up a campsite. They moved into a tent about half a mile from where the Tates lived.

They slept on canvas cots and ate mostly canned and packaged foods. They also had eggs, bacon, and occasionally a chicken. Orville prepared the meals. Wilbur did the dishwashing.

In a letter to Katharine, Orville told her what Kitty Hawk was like. "At any time we look out of the tent door, we can see an eagle flapping its way over head [and] buzzards by the dozen...," Orville wrote.

"But the sand! The sand is the greatest thing in Kitty Hawk, and soon will be the only thing. The sea has washed and the wind blown millions and millions of loads of sand up in heaps along the coast, completely covering houses and forest."

In their first tests, the brothers flew the glider as a kite. Each held lines that operated controls as their craft floated in the sky.

After about two weeks, Wilbur decided to try his hand as a pilot. He lay flat on the lower wing, his hands grasping the elevator. Orville and Bill Tate each took hold of a wingtip and trotted forward with the machine until the glider began to lift.

With the aid of strong winds, it climbed to an altitude of about fifteen feet. Wilbur was elated. Suddenly the glider began to make jerky moves.

"Let me down!" Wilbur yelled.

Orville and Bill Tate, holding the control lines, guided the craft to a soft landing.

Once back on the ground, Wilbur explained why

The Wrights first flew their glider as a kite, with each of the brothers holding lines that controlled the aircraft.

he had cut short the flight. "I promised Pop I'd take care of myself," he said.

The testing continued. Sometimes the brothers flew the glider as an unmanned kite. Other times they weighed down the craft with heavy chains. This was to test the glider's ability to carry loads of various sizes.

One day the brothers were making adjustments to

the aircraft as it rested on the sand. A sudden gust of wind caught the underside of the wings. The brothers watched in horror as the wind lifted the craft from the ground, flipped it over, and then slammed it down hard.

Part of the glider's wooden frame was smashed. Wires snapped. Three days of repair work followed.

Before the brothers returned to Dayton, they moved their test site from the beach at Kitty Hawk to Kill Devil Hills. About four miles south of their camp, Kill Devil Hills was the name that had been given to three huge sand dunes that had been formed by the wind.

In 1900, on their first trip to Kitty Hawk, North Carolina, the Wright brothers set up camp on this near-empty windswept beach.

Big Kill Devil Hill, the tallest of the hills of sand, was almost 100 feet in height. The brothers decided to use the smooth, slanting sides of Big Kill Devil Hill to launch the glider.

One day Wilbur made about a dozen flights from the top of Big Kill Devil Hill. He would lie down in the center of the lower wing. Then Orville and Bill Tate would each grasp a wingtip and race down the slope until the glider had taken to the air.

Some of Wilbur's glides were 300 to 400 feet in length. They lasted as long as fifteen seconds.

Toward the end of October, the brothers returned to Dayton. They left the glider behind, telling Bill Tate that it was his if he wanted it. Mrs. Tate salvaged the cotton cloth from the wings. From it she made dresses for her two young daughters.

Looking back, Orville and Wilbur were pleased. They realized that they had outdone what had been achieved by Otto Lilienthal and Samuel Langley. Never before had a person been carried through the air while lying between a pair of wings.

Orville summed up how they felt. He said that

they were happy "to be able to return [home] without having our pet theories completely knocked in the head. . . ." He also said that they were grateful that their brains had not been "dashed out" during the experience.

1 9 0 1

AFTER RETURNING TO DAYTON FROM the Outer Banks, the Wrights began planning a bigger and better glider. By mid-May 1901, the new machine was completed.

Like the earlier craft, it was a biplane. Each of its two wings was twenty-two feet long and seven feet from front to back. It weighed almost 100 pounds. It was the biggest glider ever built.

An important change was included. In the 1900 glider, the pilot controlled the twisting of the wings, called wing warping, with his feet. But in the new machine, the pilot's hips were enclosed in a wooden cradle on the lower wing. By shifting his hips in one direction or the other, the pilot could twist one wing up and the other down.

The brothers returned to the Outer Banks of North Carolina on July 10, 1901. They decided to set up camp near the dunes at Kill Devil Hills, not Kitty Hawk. Again they lived in a tent. Next to it they built a large wooden shed to shelter the glider.

At about the time the shed was completed, a visitor named Edward Huffaker arrived. The Wrights had been expecting him. A friend of Octave Chanute's, Huffaker was at work on a glider of his own. He hoped to test it at Kill Devil Hills. Chanute himself and another friend of his also visited the Wrights' campsite that year.

Troubles struck the Wrights during their stay that year. At first there were heavy rains that lasted for a week. There was little the Wrights could do. They were like prisoners in their tent.

When the rains finally stopped, mosquitoes attacked the campers. They came, as Orville noted, "in a mighty cloud, almost darkening the sun."

Orville added, "There was no escape. The sand and grass and trees and hills and everything was crawling with them. They chewed us clean through our underwear and socks. Lumps began swelling all over my body like hen's eggs."

To drive off the mosquitoes, they gathered old tree stumps and burned them. The thick smoke was easier to put up with than the insects.

Once they began to test the glider, there were more serious problems. On their first attempt to get the machine into the air, it nose-dived into the sand. When they finally got the aircraft to fly, it continued to be a disappointment.

Wilbur was the pilot. Although one of his glides was 315 feet long and lasted nineteen seconds, most of the time he struggled. Twice the glider stopped dead in the air. Fortunately, the machine dropped straight down without injuring him. It was scary. As Orville mentioned in a letter to Katharine, "this is precisely the fix [that] Lilienthal got into when he was killed."

The brothers spent several days tinkering with the glider. They wanted to improve Wilbur's ability to control it.

When Wilbur tested the rebuilt machine, he

Bill Tate (left) and Bill's half brother Dan (right) help in launching the 1901 glider. Wilbur is the pilot.

made several successful flights. One covered 389 feet.

There was still a problem with wing warping. When the wings were warped for a short span of time, the system worked well. Wilbur could keep the aircraft balanced in the sky. But when he tried warping for a long period, the machine spun out of control.

Once, when he dropped the left wing, he could

not raise it. The glider slipped to the left, then crashed into the sand. Wilbur was thrown forward, slamming into the elevator. He came out of the accident with a bruised nose, a black eye, and cuts on his face.

During the early weeks of August, the brothers continued to test their machine. Nothing much was accomplished. Then more rains came. They decided to close down their camp and return home.

The brothers were wrapped in gloom on their train ride home. The year before had been much different. They had left Kitty Hawk in high spirits. But in 1901, instead of solving problems, they seemed to have created new ones.

They were puzzled. They were depressed.

"When we left Kitty Hawk at the end of 1901 ...," Wilbur would later write, "we considered our experiments a failure. At this time I made the prediction that men would sometime fly, but that it would not be within our lifetime."

1 9 0 2

AT HOME, ORVILLE AND WILBUR kept looking back at their two years of glider testing at the Outer Banks. They began to suspect what had gone wrong. In designing their gliders, they had relied too heavily on information from others. The facts and figures from Lilienthal and Chanute were filled with errors.

When it came to scientific data of the past, the Wrights agreed to "cast it all aside." They would instead "rely on [their] own intelligence."

To develop their own facts and figures, the Wrights built a boxlike structure. It was six feet long and sixteen inches wide. A metal fan provided a stream of air through the box. At the top, there was a glass window to view the inside. This was the world's first wind tunnel.

Model aircraft, or parts of aircraft, could be placed within the tunnel. By looking through the viewing window, one could see how they reacted to the wind's flow.

In their bicycle workshop, the brothers made some 150 miniature metal wings of assorted sizes and shapes. Each of the wings was tested in the wind tunnel. The experimenting continued for weeks.

The work filled the brothers with excitement. "Wilbur and I could hardly wait for morning to come," Orville wrote, "to get at something that interested us."

The wind-tunnel tests helped the Wrights to decide how to build their new glider. It was bigger than their earlier gliders. But it was also more graceful looking.

The wings—thirty-two feet long, five feet deep— were longer and narrower. They were also shaped differently. Each wing had a rounded forward edge. This design would provide more upward lift and help to overcome the control problems of the 1901 machine.

By the end of August 1902, the Wrights were back on the Outer Banks off the coast of North Carolina. They spent the first few days getting their camp at Kill Devil Hills in shape. They decided to enlarge the wooden shed that they had built the year before. They wanted to be able to sleep in it rather than in a tent.

"We fitted our living arrangements much more comfortably than last year," Wilbur said in a letter to Katharine. "Our kitchen is immensely improved, and then we have made beds on the second floor and now sleep aloft [high up]. It is an improvement over cots."

By September 19, the glider had been assembled and was ready for testing. Dan Tate, Bill Tate's half brother, helped them carry the aircraft to Little Kill Devil Hill, the smallest of the Kill Devil Hills. There they flew it as a kite, with no pilot aboard. The aircraft soared in splendid fashion.

The next day they took the machine to the

Orville, at the controls of the 1902 glider, gets a helping hand from Wilbur (left) and Dan Tate.

longer and steeper slopes of Big Kill Devil Hill. Wilbur made the first glides of the year, testing the new controls.

Orville had not flown before so he took a turn at a few short glides.

One of Orville's early flights almost ended in disaster. "I was sailing along smoothly without any trouble . . . ," Orville wrote, "when I noticed that one wing was getting a little too high and that the machine was sliding off in the opposite direction. . . ."

Orville quickly shifted his hips in an effort to

balance the aircraft. But it didn't respond. Instead, the machine nosed up, then stalled, and toppled backward onto the sand. "The result," Orville wrote, "was a heap of flying machine, cloth, and sticks in a heap, with me in the center without a bruise or scratch."

The brothers repaired the damage. The machine was back in the air a week later.

When the weather was good and the wind favorable, they made as many as twenty-five flights a day. A few flights were longer than 500 feet.

Still, there was a serious problem. At times the glider would fall sideways toward the ground. The pilot would seek to balance the aircraft, but would fail. A bone-jarring crash would result.

Lying awake one night after Wilbur had gone to sleep, Orville hit upon what might be a solution. He announced it to Wilbur at breakfast the next morning. Make the tail movable, he suggested. Make the tail swing to the right or left. This would give the pilot more control.

Wilbur listened carefully. He liked the idea.

Then Wilbur had a suggestion of his own. Link the movable tail to the wing-warping system. Then, when the pilot shifted his hips to warp the wings, he would move the tail at the same time. The brothers began working on the new tail system that very day.

By this time, Lorin, the oldest of the Wright siblings, had arrived at the camp. He was eager to see what progress his brothers were making. Octave Chanute and two of his friends were also visiting.

The brothers' most successful flights were made after their guests had left. Each day from dawn to dusk they were in the air. One perfect flight followed another. One of Wilbur's flights covered 622½ feet and lasted twenty-six seconds. In terms of both distance and time, that flight was a record setter.

Orville was filled with joy. "In two days, we made over 250 glides," he said in a letter to Katharine, "or more than we made all together up to the time Lorin left.

"Day before yesterday, we had a wind of . . . about 30 miles per hour, and glided in it without any trouble. That was the highest wind a gliding

With their 1902 glider, the Wrights established records for time aloft and distance covered. Wilbur is the pilot here.

machine was ever in, so that we now hold all the records!"

The records that were set tell only part of the story. With their 1902 glider, the Wright brothers had solved the basic problems of flight.

They were able to control up-and-down movement. They were also able to make smooth turns and keep the aircraft balanced.

As the end of October 1902 neared, the brothers packed to leave camp. Wilbur and Orville knew they would be back the following year. They were excited about what they planned to do next. They would build a glider with an engine—a powered flying machine.

THE *FLYER*

TO DRIVE THEIR NEW AIRCRAFT forward through the air, the Wrights needed an engine. It would have to be powerful. But it could weigh no more than 200 pounds.

Wilbur wrote to several companies that made car motors. Could they supply them with the engine that they needed? None of the companies seemed interested.

The brothers realized they were going to have to build the engine themselves. They were lucky to have Charlie Taylor to help them. Taylor, who now managed the bicycle shop, was skilled at making machine parts.

"One of us would sketch out the part we were talking about...," Taylor explained. From these simple drawings, each engine part was roughed out, then crafted into its final form. In six weeks, the engine was ready for testing.

The engine alone could not drive their aircraft through the air by itself. The Wrights' flying machine also required a propeller.

Samuel Langley and other aviation pioneers had given little thought to propeller design. If the Wrights wanted an effective propeller, they would have to design it themselves.

It was no easy matter. "What at first seemed a simple problem became more complex the longer we studied it," Orville wrote.

After many weeks of study and testing, the brothers worked out the correct propeller size and the proper angle for each blade. They decided their aircraft needed two propellers, not one. They were to be mounted behind the wings. One would spin clockwise, the other counterclockwise.

Orville at work assembling the 1903 aircraft in the Flyer's hangar at Kill Devil Hills.

The brothers had no trouble devising a method of connecting the propellers to the engine. They drew upon their experience with bicycles.

Pedal power drives a bicycle. The pedal system is linked to the rear wheel by a chain whose links fit into toothed wheels called sprockets.

The Wrights used a similar hookup in their new aircraft. Chains and sprockets delivered the engine's power to each of the propellers.

The Flyer's engine weighed about 200 pounds and delivered 12 horsepower.

At the same time that they were working on their engine and propellers, the brothers were assembling the aircraft itself. It was to be the biggest machine yet. It would have a wingspan of forty feet, four inches. The wings measured six feet, six inches from front to back. The brothers called the aircraft the *Flyer*.

The brothers mounted the engine on the lower wing. They placed it just to the right of where the pilot was to lie. There was a safety reason for this. In case of a crash, the engine would not fall on the pilot.

During the months that they worked on the aircraft, Orville often wrote to Octave Chanute. He told him they were building a machine "much larger and about twice as heavy" as the 1902 glider.

In one of his replies, Chanute remarked, "I think you had better patent your improvements."

The Wrights were well aware of the importance of getting a patent to protect their ideas. A patent is a legal right that the government gives to an inventor. The inventor then becomes the only person allowed to make or sell the new invention. A patent would help to prevent the Wrights' ideas from being copied.

On March 23, 1903, the Wrights applied for their first patent. It was for their wing-warping system.

The government's response disappointed the brothers. They were told their drawings were incomplete. Their description of wing warping was said to be "vague and indefinite."

The brothers tried a second time. Again the patent office denied their request.

The rejections puzzled the Wrights. It also caused them some worry. The brothers had a right to feel troubled. Protecting their inventions would be a problem for years to come.

SUCCESS

WHEN ORVILLE AND WILBUR returned to the Outer Banks late in September 1903, they had a different goal than their goals in past years. Their plan had always been to experiment and learn. They felt differently now. They just wanted to get the *Flyer* into the air for a controlled flight of good distance.

Once the crates that held the *Flyer* arrived, Wilbur and Orville began assembling the aircraft. When they began testing the engine, they found problems with the propellers. Eventually, Orville had to return to Dayton to supervise their remaking. It was mid-December before he was back in Kitty Hawk with the new propellers.

Winter was now close at hand. Each morning the water in their washbasin was frozen. At night, the brothers piled on the blankets. In a letter home, Wilbur noted that "last year [we had] 1, 2, 3 and 4 blanket nights. We now have 5 blanket nights, and 5 blankets & 2 quilts. Next come 5 blankets, 2 quilts & fire; then 5, 2, fire, & hot water jug."

By Monday, December 14, the brothers were ready to test the *Flyer* for the first time. To help ease the plane into the air on takeoffs, they built a rail system. It consisted of a sixty-foot wooden track, made in fifteen-foot sections. They nailed a thin metal strip to the top of the track.

For takeoffs, the *Flyer* would be placed atop a small two-wheeled cart that ran along the track. With its propellers spinning, the *Flyer* would travel along the rail on the cart. Once it had gained enough speed, the *Flyer* would lift into the air, leaving the cart behind.

As the brothers began preparing for the first flight, they realized the wind was not strong enough for the *Flyer* to take off from level ground. They decided to

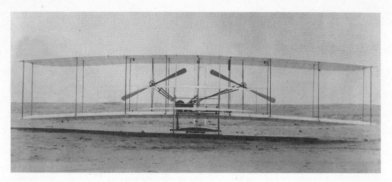

A front view of the 1903 aircraft. The two propellers were hand-crafted by the Wrights.

move the starting track and the *Flyer* to Big Kill Devil Hill for a downhill start.

At 1:30 that afternoon, the brothers hung a big red flag from the side of their workshop. The flag was a signal to the men at the lifesaving station that a flight was about to be attempted. It implied that they could use some help. Before long, several men and two little boys ambled down the beach to the launch site.

The lifesavers helped move the starting track and the *Flyer* about a quarter of a mile to Big Kill Devil Hill. It was hard work.

By mid-afternoon, the brothers were ready. The

Flyer was poised at the end of the track that ran down the sloping side of Big Kill Devil Hill. They started the engine.

The loud clatter blotted out all conversation. One had to yell to be heard.

Both brothers were confident of success. As Orville later recalled, "With the slope of the track ...and the machine starting directly into the wind, we did not anticipate any trouble getting up flying speed...."

Who would be the pilot? To decide, the brothers flipped a coin. Wilbur won. He lay down on the lower wing. Once he felt comfortable, he released the wire that held the aircraft in place. Noisily, the 605-pound *Flyer* raced down the track and lifted into the air.

Once the craft began climbing, it rose at too sharp an angle. It slowed, stopped, then dove toward the ground. According to Orville's stopwatch, Wilbur was in the air for only three and a half seconds.

"The wind was a little to one side and the track was not exactly straight down hill," Wilbur was later to explain in a letter to the family. These factors, he said, "caused the start to be more difficult than it would otherwise have been."

Wilbur admitted he had made in an error in judgment. He had turned up too suddenly. "Before I could correct the error," he said, "the machine started to come down...."

Despite the lack of success, the brothers felt good about the test. "The experiment demonstrated that the method adopted for launching the machine was a safe and practical one," Wilbur wrote. "On the whole, we were much pleased."

Wilbur came out of the first attempt without injury. Unfortunately, one of the plane's ski-like landing runners, called skids, was cracked. There was also some other minor damage. It took two days to make the repairs.

On Thursday, December 17, the brothers were ready to try again. The day was clear and very cold. Ice sheeted the puddles of standing water.

A blustery wind swept out of the north. Any attempt to fly would be difficult. The brothers hoped the wind would die down. But when it did not, they decided they would try anyway.

Once again they hung out their signal flag for the men at the lifesaving station. Then they began laying down the launching rail on level ground not far from the shed they used as a workshop.

By the time the starting track was in place, several men from the lifesaving station had arrived. They helped get the *Flyer* ready for the launch.

Since Wilbur had been the pilot on the first attempt, it was now Orville's turn. He climbed into place on the lower wing. He was wearing a dark suit, a stiff collar, and a necktie.

"After running the motor a few minutes to heat it up," Orville later wrote, "I released the wire that held the machine to the track, and the machine started forward in the wind. Wilbur ran at the side of the machine, holding the wing to balance it on the track."

Heading into a strong wind that gusted up to twenty-seven miles an hour, the plane moved slowly. Wilbur had no trouble keeping up with it. As

This famous photograph, taken on December 17, 1903, pictures the first manned flight in a heavier-than-air machine. Orville is the pilot. Wilbur is shown running alongside the aircraft.

the aircraft rose from the track, the men from the lifesaving station let out a small cheer.

Once airborne, the *Flyer* lurched about crazily. "The course of the flight up and down was exceedingly erratic [uncertain]...," Orville wrote, "the machine would rise suddenly to about ten feet and then as suddenly dart for the ground."

The flight lasted twelve seconds. The *Flyer*

traveled 120 feet. But Orville was quick to realize its significance. It was, he later noted, "the first in the history of the world in which a machine carrying a man had raised itself by its own power into the air in full flight, had sailed forward without reduction of speed, and had finally landed at a point from which it started."

The brothers hauled the *Flyer* back to the starting point for another try. Everyone was very cold by this time. They went inside the Wrights' living quarters to get warm.

Wilbur was at the controls for the second flight that day. It also lasted twelve seconds. But it was longer, stretching 175 feet.

Twenty minutes later, Orville was the pilot for the third flight. "This one was steadier than the first," Orville noted. He covered 200 feet in fifteen seconds.

At around noon, Wilbur tried again. It was the last flight of the day. It was also the most impressive. Wilbur kept the *Flyer* in the air for fifty-nine seconds. He traveled 852 feet.

Once more, the men carried the aircraft back to

the starting point. As the next flight was being discussed, a sudden gust of wind caught the underside of the wings and rolled the plane backward. Wires snapped. Wooden parts splintered. The engine was pulled from its mount.

Major repairs were needed. The brothers decided to end testing and ship the aircraft's remains back to Dayton.

That afternoon, Orville and Wilbur walked four miles up the beach to Kitty Hawk. At the weather station there, they sent a telegram to their father, announcing that they had launched their machine and that it had actually flown.

The message was a simple one. "Success four flights Thursday," it began. Success was indeed the right word. What the Wright brothers had done was realize a goal that had challenged people for centuries.

AT HUFFMAN
PRAIRIE

THEIR SUCCESS AT KILL DEVIL HILLS in 1903 marked an important turning point in the lives of the Wright brothers. They decided that flying would no longer be a mere hobby, a sideline.

The Wrights put the day-to-day operation of the bicycle shop in the hands of Charlie Taylor. They began to devote themselves to flying on a full-time basis. Their goal became to produce an airplane that could do much more than make brief, straight-line hops.

"They wanted a new one built right away," Charlie Taylor recalled.

The Wrights' new aircraft was similar to the

1903 machine, but it had a stronger body and wings. Its engine had a good deal more power. It was called *Flyer II*.

To test the machine, the brothers launched a search for a new site. Kitty Hawk was too far away, they had decided. Getting there was too expensive. They settled upon Huffman Prairie, a spacious cow pasture about eight miles east of their home in Dayton.

"We are in a large meadow of about 100 acres," Orville said in a letter to Octave Chanute. "It is skirted on the west and north by trees." The trees could be a hazard to a low-flying airplane. But Orville did not consider this to be "anything serious."

At first, the Wrights made little progress at Huffman Prairie. Their starting track had worked well on the long flat beaches of the Outer Banks. But it was a chore to lay the track on the bumpy pasture.

When they did manage to get *Flyer II* into the air, it didn't stay there very long. After several weeks, all

The Wrights launched Flyer II *from this wooden starting track.*

they had to show for their efforts was a series of short flights.

Their biggest problem was a lack of decent wind. "We were usually up against a rain storm, a dead calm, or a wind blowing at right angles to the track," Wilbur wrote.

They overcame the wind problem by building a clever launching system. They first constructed a twenty-foot tower behind the track's starting point. A 1,600-pound weight was raised to the top of the

Orville and Wilbur with Flyer II *at Huffman Prairie in May 1904.*

tower. *Flyer II*, mounted on its starting track, was attached to the weight by a rope-and-pulley system.

When the weight was dropped, the rope pulled the *Flyer* along the track. By the time the aircraft reached the track's end, it was traveling at flying speed and lifted into the air.

With the new launching system, the Wrights were able to make many more flights. The flights soon got longer. They became more carefully controlled. By mid-September 1904, the brothers were making flights of up to half a mile. They were also making their first full turns in the air.

On September 20, Wilbur flew a complete circle in the sky. A Medina, Ohio, beekeeper named Amos Root witnessed the flight and reported what he saw. "When it first turned the circle, and came near the starting point, I was right in front of it; and I said then, and I believe still, it was one of the grandest sights, if not the grandest sight, of my life. Imagine a locomotive that has left its track, and is climbing up in the air right toward you—a locomotive without any wheels, we will say, but with white wings instead . . . coming right toward you. . . ."

In the weeks that followed, the brothers continued to fly complete circles. On November 9, Wilbur circled the airfield four times in five minutes. It was the longest flight of 1904.

In the summer of 1905, the Wrights began testing a new and improved model of their aircraft. They had spectacular success with it. Three-, four-, and five-minute flights became routine.

On October 5, 1905, Wilbur shattered all records.

He circled the field thirty times in thirty-nine minutes. The flight covered a distance of twenty-four and a half miles.

The third Wright *Flyer* was the world's first practical airplane. *Practical*, says the dictionary, means "sound, efficient, realistic." The new craft was all of these.

The Wrights were fully aware of what they had succeeded in doing. As Wilbur told a friend, they had transformed flying "from the realm of scientific problems to that of useful arts." To put it another way, the Wrights had launched the age of flight.

SHOWING
THE WORLD

THE WORLD TOOK LITTLE NOTICE OF what the Wrights had achieved at Kill Devil Hills and Huffman Prairie. The brothers themselves were partly to blame for this. They feared their ideas would be stolen and copied. So they were closemouthed about what they had done. They did not want publicity.

Octave Chanute felt differently. If the brothers were really capable of making long flights, they should tell the world. He urged them to demonstrate what they had achieved before the largest possible audience. But the Wrights had no thought of staging flights for the public.

Their attitude hurt them when they tried to

sell their machine. They would not demonstrate their aircraft. They would not even let buyers see it until contracts were signed.

The Wrights believed it was their duty to give the U.S. Army the first chance to buy their invention. But army officials found it hard to believe that a flying machine really existed. They asked for detailed drawings and descriptions. Or they wanted a chance to see the aircraft in operation. The Wrights refused.

On May 22, 1906, the United States government finally granted the Wrights the patent they had been seeking. It covered most of the systems used to control the aircraft in flight.

But as far as the brothers were concerned, the patent changed nothing. It did not guarantee them protection, they felt. Plenty of inventors with patents had had their ideas stolen.

The brothers stuck to their decision not to fly until someone agreed to pay a fair price for their invention. As a result, they did not take to the air for three years.

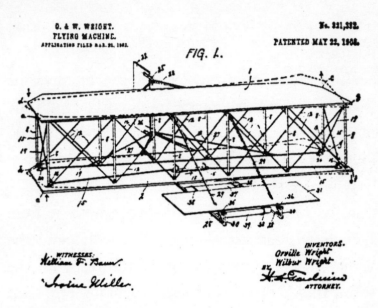

O. & W. WRIGHT.
FLYING MACHINE.
APPLICATION FILED MAR. 21, 1903.

No. 821,332.

PATENTED MAY 22, 1906.

FIG. 1.

WITNESSES:
William F. Bauer.
Irene Miller.

INVENTORS.
Orville Wright
Wilbur Wright
BY
H. A. Toulmin
ATTORNEY.

On May 22, 1906, the Wrights were granted a government patent for their 1903 "flying machine."

They remained in Dayton, designing a new and improved model of their aircraft. They called it the *Wright Type A Flyer*.

It had several changes. The Wrights had learned that long flights while lying flat were hard on the pilot. In the *Type A Flyer*, the pilot was seated for the first time. The aircraft also boasted a second seat for a passenger. Hand levers for controlling up-and-down movement and for turning were other advances.

With the U.S. Army out of the picture, the Wrights traveled to Europe in an effort to sell the machine. The governments of Britain, France, and Germany showed interest. The brothers, however, were unable to complete a sale.

In November 1907, on the voyage home from Europe, Wilbur felt gloomy. "We will spend the winter getting some more machines ready for the spring trade," he said in a letter to his father. "Then we will probably put out a sign, 'Opening day, all goods below cost.'"

Reduced prices were never necessary. Soon after Wilbur's return to America, the U.S. Army had a change of heart. Weeks of negotiations followed. In February 1908, the brothers signed a contract with the army. Under its terms, they agreed to provide a flying machine "capable of carrying two men and sufficient fuel supplies for a flight of 125 miles, with a speed of at least forty miles an hour."

A month later there was more good news. The

French had also become seriously interested in Wright airplanes. The brothers signed a contract with a company that was to manufacture Wright *Flyers* in France.

Both contracts called for the Wrights to stage demonstration flights. The brothers would soon be flying again. But their skills had grown rusty. They returned to Kitty Hawk for some practice flights and to test the *Type A Flyer.*

Afterward, Wilbur made plans to journey alone to France to demonstrate the *Flyer* there. Orville would conduct the test flights for the U.S. Army in Virginia.

In France, Wilbur found that the brothers' unwillingness to fly had cast great doubts about their success. The French considered themselves to be the leaders in aviation research. By the summer of 1908, French aviators had made flights that lasted more than twenty minutes. But these were shaky attempts at best. The French had not mastered the ability to control an aircraft in the sky.

The French questioned the Wrights without

letup. The Paris edition of the *New York Herald* ran an editorial with the headline "FLIERS OR LIARS." Wilbur, however, had greater problems than the doubting French. The *Flyer*'s airframe was seriously damaged in shipment. Weeks had to be spent repairing broken pieces.

Language differences made matters worse. Wilbur did not speak French. His mechanics spoke no English. He had to perform most major tasks himself. The wing assembly was one. "I was the only one strong enough in the fingers to pull the wires together tight," he wrote, "so I had all the sewing to do myself." The result was "hands [that] were about raw when I was not half done."

By August 8, Wilbur was ready to make the Wrights' first public flight. The site was a small racecourse near the town of Le Mans, about 120 miles southwest of Paris.

A small crowd that included a number of French airmen had turned out. They watched quietly as workers mounted the *Flyer* onto the starting rail. Then the workers connected the aircraft by a long rope to the huge weight atop of the starting tower. It was like the starting tower the Wrights had used at Huffman Prairie.

Wilbur climbed into the pilot's seat. He signaled for the weight to be released. The *Flyer* hurried down the track, then lifted gracefully into the air. A cheer went up from the crowd.

Climbing higher, Wilbur tilted one wing up and the other down, banking into a turn. The spectators oohed and aahed. They had never seen a banked turn before.

Wilbur circled the racecourse a second time before bringing the *Flyer* down for a smooth landing. The crowd rushed out onto the field to surround the aircraft and shake Wilbur's hand.

In the week that followed, Wilbur flew eight more times at Le Mans. In his best showing, he completed seven circuits of the track. He stayed aloft for more than eight minutes.

The French, indeed all Europeans, needed no further proof. The *London Daily Mirror* saluted the *Flyer* as "THE MOST WONDERFUL FLYING MACHINE

Mrs. Hart Berg, the first woman passenger in an airplane, and Wilbur before their historic flight made on October 7, 1908.

EVER MADE." The newspaper awarded the Wrights "first place in the history of flying machines."

The French newspaper *Le Figaro* was also caught in the excitement. "I have seen them! Yes!" said a reporter. "I have seen Wilbur Wright and his great white bird, the beautiful mechanical bird . . . there is no doubt! Wilbur and Orville Wright have well and truly flown."

Wilbur made several other news-making flights in

France that summer. On no less than sixty occasions, he took up passengers.

Meanwhile, on the other side of the Atlantic, Orville was preparing to test another *Flyer* for the U.S. Army. In a letter to Orville, Wilbur advised his younger brother to "be awfully careful in beginning practice and go slowly."

HEROES

W HILE WILBUR DAZZLED EUROPE with his flying feats, Orville was test-flying another Wright aircraft for the U.S. Army from the parade grounds at Fort Myer, Virginia, near Washington, D.C. Like his brother, Orville was soon making headlines.

Orville started slowly, as Wilbur suggested. The first time he took to the air, he flew only a circle and a half above the parade ground, staying aloft for not much more than a minute.

Before long, however, he was setting records for both distance and endurance. Each day spectators by the hundreds made the trip from Washington to watch Orville fly.

Early in September 1908, Orville set a record

of nine minutes, six and half seconds for a flight with a passenger. On September 17, he was set to make another passenger flight. Lieutenant Thomas Selfridge of the U.S. Army would be seated next to him.

The flight began without any problems. Orville circled the parade ground twice. As he began a third circuit, one of the *Flyer*'s propellers struck a wire that held a part of the tail in place. The propeller cracked, causing it to lose power.

Trouble loomed. "I heard a light tapping in the rear of the machine," Orville later wrote. "I suppose it was not over two or three seconds from the time the first taps were heard, till two big thumps, which gave the machine a terrible shaking, showed that something had broken."

Orville cut the engine and struggled to put the aircraft into a gentle glide. Instead, the plane headed straight down.

The *Flyer* slammed into the ground and toppled over onto its back. Orville and Selfridge were buried in the wreckage. Selfridge died in the crash. His

Orville is carried on a stretcher after his ill-fated flight of September 17, 1908, which brought death to Lieutenant Thomas Selfridge, his passenger.

death was the first in a powered airplane. Orville survived, but he had facial cuts, a broken leg, several cracked ribs, and an injured back.

Wilbur, in France at the time, blamed himself for the accident. In a letter to Katharine, he declared, "I cannot help thinking over and over again, 'If I had been there, it would not have happened....' It was not right to leave Orville to undertake such a task alone."

Almost a year passed before Orville felt well enough to fly again. He was seldom without back pain for the rest of his life. Sometimes the pain was so bad it sent him to bed for days at a time.

In January 1909, Orville and Katharine sailed for France to join Wilbur there. After a reunion in Paris, the three journeyed south to Pau, a resort town not far from the Spanish border. Wilbur was training French pilots there.

In the months that followed, a steady stream of notables traveled to Pau to witness Wilbur's flights. King Alfonso XIII of Spain and Edward VII of England were among those who made the trek. "Kings," Katharine told a reporter, "are just like other nice, well-bred people."

From Pau, the Wrights went on to Rome. There, Wilbur made demonstration flights and trained Italian aviators.

After Italy, the Wrights traveled to England. On May 4, 1909, the trio sailed for New York. As their ocean liner entered New York Harbor, a fleet of small boats awaited them. Ships in the harbor

Kings, queens, and heads of state were among those who traveled to Pau to watch Wilbur's demonstration flights. King Alfonso XIII of Spain (left) was one of the royal visitors.

saluted them with bells, whistles, and signal flags. Newspapers gave them front-page coverage.

New York City officials planned to stage welcoming festivities to honor the Wrights. Meanwhile, the people of Dayton were planning their own ceremony.

The Wrights favored Dayton. They asked New

York officials to put aside their plans. They said they wished to return to Dayton as quickly as possible.

The Wrights looked upon all such festivities as a waste of time. They had the new *Flyer* on their minds. They were eager to complete work on the aircraft, take it to Virginia, and fly it for the army at Fort Myer.

Nevertheless, on June 17 and 18, the brothers had no choice but to take part in the Dayton celebration. There were parades, band concerts, and fireworks. The brothers received gold medals—from the city of Dayton, the state of Ohio, and the U.S. Congress.

During the summer of 1909, the brothers began testing their new aircraft for the army at Fort Myer. Orville did all of the flying.

One of the flights took the form of a two-man speed test. The army had agreed to pay $25,000 for the *Flyer* if Orville could manage a speed of forty miles an hour. Orville did better. His average speed was forty-two and a half miles an hour. The feat

Wilbur (left) and Orville on the porch steps of their Dayton home in June 1909.

earned the Wrights a bonus of $5,000 in the purchase price of the aircraft.

Late in September 1909, Wilbur made his first public flights in the United States. They took place in New York City.

Wilbur planned to take off from Governors Island at the southern tip of Manhattan. He would then fly over New York Harbor. Wilbur had never flown over water before. He had a red canoe installed between the plane's skids, the runners used to help landing. He did this in case he had to make an emergency landing in the harbor. During the flight, Wilbur circled the Statue of Liberty at its waist, canoe and all.

The following week, Wilbur flew about ten miles up the Hudson River, then back. About a million New Yorkers watched in awe.

Early in November, Wilbur's name was in the headlines again. Taking off from a spacious cow pasture at College Park, Maryland, he flew at the record speed of forty-six miles an hour. No one realized it at the time, but it was Wilbur's last public flight.

CHAPTER 14

"A SHORT LIFE..."

BEFORE 1909 ENDED, THE WRIGHT brothers formed their own company to build and sell their aircraft. It was called the Wright Company. Wilbur would serve as president, Orville, as a vice president.

The Wrights hoped to be able to turn over the day-to-day operation of the company to skilled managers. Doing so would leave them free to develop advanced models of their aircraft.

The future seemed bright. But little by little, the brothers' worst fears were beginning to be realized. Once they had begun to show their airplanes in public, it became easy for other aircraft makers to copy their ideas. And many did.

The Wrights felt this was wrong. They did not want others earning profits at their expense. When someone used one of their inventions, the Wright brothers felt they should be paid. So began a long period of bitter lawsuits against rival inventors whom the Wrights accused of copying ideas that they had patented.

Glenn Hammond Curtiss was their first target. Like the Wrights, Curtiss had been a bicycle mechanic. He later became well known as a motorcycle racer. Curtiss also invented a powerful, lightweight engine that was ideal for aircraft.

Curtiss was a member of the Aerial Experiment Association. The group built a number of aircraft to compete with the Wright *Flyers*.

Early in 1910, the Wrights brought a lawsuit against Curtiss. They claimed that his method of controlling his aircraft was based on their wing-warping system. The court ordered Curtiss to stop making and selling airplanes.

The Wrights were loudly criticized for bringing lawsuits against Curtiss and others. They were said to be smothering aircraft development in America. They were called greedy.

The brothers received an angry letter from Octave Chanute. "Your usually sound judgment," Chanute said, "has been warped by your desire for great wealth."

The Wrights rejected the idea that they were money-hungry. All they sought was fairness, they said.

Orville was not eager to become involved in the legal quarrels. He preferred to spend his time testing the latest Wright aircraft at Huffman Prairie. He also taught would-be pilots to fly.

Many of Orville's students went on to take part in flying meets and aerial exhibitions, which had become popular. In these, daredevil pilots risked their lives for prize money.

Calbraith Rodgers was one of the graduates of the Wrights' flying school at Huffman Prairie. Rodgers won legendary fame by completing America's first coast-to-coast flight. During the journey, the six-foot-four, 200-pound Rodgers piloted a *Wright*

Calbraith Rodgers, piloting a Wright Flyer *named the* Vin Fiz, *takes off from Sheepshead Bay in Brooklyn, New York, to begin what was to be the first coast-to-coast flight across the United States.*

Model EX, an aircraft built for exhibition flights. He called it the *Vin Fiz*. That was the name of a new grape drink that helped to sponsor the flight.

The historic flight took eighty-four days. Rodgers left Sheepshead Bay in Brooklyn, New York, on September 17, 1911. A cheering crowd greeted him on arrival in Long Beach, California, on December 10. He had flown 4,231 miles. He made sixty-eight landings and takeoffs. He crash-landed nine times, suffering a broken ankle, a twisted back, and a slight concussion.

Not long after Rodgers completed his historic flight to the Pacific coast, Orville made a return trip to Kitty Hawk. Lorin Wright, his ten-year-old son Horace, and a British pilot named Alexander Ogilvie went with Orville.

Wilbur and Orville had developed a device that would automatically control an aircraft once it was in the air. Orville designed a glider in which the control system could be tested.

The new glider was a triumph. On October 24, 1911, Orville remained aloft in the unpowered aircraft for nine minutes, forty-five seconds—a record. It remained a record for ten years.

Wilbur, meanwhile, was continuing with the patent lawsuits. He traveled to Europe to testify in court. Back in the United States, he made frequent trips from Dayton to New York. There the case against Curtiss was being tried.

The constant travel and the pressure of his court

Orville test-flies his glider over the beach at Kill Devil Hills in 1911.

appearances were hard on Wilbur's health. He often appeared pale and tired.

In April 1912, Wilbur fell ill while on a trip to Boston. When he arrived back home early in May, he felt better. But then he developed a high fever.

Doctors found that Wilbur had typhoid fever, a common disease of the time. Eating spoiled food or drinking polluted water can cause typhoid fever.

Wilbur's condition kept getting worse. He was unconscious much of the time.

"Wilbur is sinking," Bishop Wright wrote in his diary on May 28. "The doctors have no hope for his recovery."

Wilbur died on May 30, 1912. He was forty-five years old.

"A short life full of consequences," wrote Bishop Wright upon his son's death. He praised Wilbur for his "unfailing intellect … great self-reliance and … great modesty."

On the day of Wilbur's passing, the Wright family received more than 1,000 telegrams expressing sympathy. At the funeral, one reporter noted that there were enough flowers to fill a freight car.

"Probably Orville and Katharine felt the loss the most," Bishop Wright noted. "They say little."

Newspapers around the world offered tributes to Wilbur. He was described as the true "inventor of the airplane." He was called the "Father of Flight" and "Conqueror of the Air."

In 1912, less than nine years after the brothers' success at Kitty Hawk, Wilbur fell sick and died. Huge crowds gathered outside the First Presbyterian Church in Dayton for his funeral.

President William Howard Taft hailed Wilbur as "the father of the great new science of aeronautics."

Orville was deeply saddened by Wilbur's passing. He took his brother's place as president of the Wright Company. But he felt uneasy in the role. In 1915, he sold his interest in the company and withdrew from the airplane business.

Most of the patent lawsuits were later decided in the Wrights' favor. Orville became a wealthy man as a result.

In the spring of 1914, Orville, Katharine, and their eighty-five-year-old father moved to a Dayton suburb. There they lived in a stately mansion named Hawthorn Hill that had been planned and designed by Orville.

Orville took great pleasure in the new home. He often entertained family members there. He tried to make even the most distant relatives feel welcome.

When World War I erupted in 1914, the airplane played a critical role. At first, aircraft were used for scouting. Orville realized the airplane could be vital in gathering information from above. "The nation with the most eyes will win the war," he said.

The United States entered the war in 1917. By that time, the airplane had become a weapon of destruction. Great numbers of planes carried out bombing raids.

Orville took note of what had happened. "The aeroplane has made war so terrible," he said, "that I

Hawthorn Hill, home to Orville Wright and the Wright family beginning in 1913.

do not believe any country will again care to start a war."

That idea was erased when World War II broke out in Europe in 1939. The war ended in 1945, shortly after American B-29 Superfortresses dropped the first atomic bomb on the Japanese city of Hiroshima. Three days later, Nagasaki was the target of a second atomic bomb.

Still, Orville remained hopeful. "I once thought the aeroplane would end wars," he said in 1945, not long after the war had ended. "I now wonder whether the aeroplane and the atomic bomb can do it."

CHAPTER 15

THE WRIGHT
BROTHERS
REMEMBERED

O N NOVEMBER 19, 1932, ORVILLE
Wright traveled once more to the
Outer Banks of North Carolina. He
was sixty-one. His hair and mustache had grown
gray.

Orville made the trip to take part in the
dedication of the Wright Brothers Memorial
Monument. The monument is a massive,
triangle-shaped chunk of granite. It is sixty feet in
height. It has wings sculpted into the sides. The
monument stands at the summit of Big Kill Devil
Hill, the ninety-foot sand dune from which the
Wrights made hundreds of their glider flights.

Wright Brothers Memorial Monument at the top of Big Kill Devil Hill in Kill Devil Hills, North Carolina, honors the brothers and marks the site of hundreds of their glider flights in 1900, 1901, and 1902.

Nearby exhibits tell the story of the Wright brothers and their historic flight. The exhibits include an exact replica of the 1903 Wright *Flyer*. More than half a million people a year visit the site.

On August 19, 1940, Orville's sixty-ninth

birthday, the city of Dayton dedicated its own monument to the Wright brothers. The monument is a thirty-foot column of pink marble. It stands on a hill overlooking Huffman Prairie. The pasture where the Wrights developed the first practical airplane is now part of Wright-Patterson Air Force Base.

At College Park, Maryland, where the Wrights test-flew early versions of their aircraft for the U.S. Army, an aviation museum welcomes visitors. Museum exhibits honor the Wrights.

The year 1943 marked the fortieth anniversary of the Wright's historic flight at Kill Devil Hills. For seventy-two-year-old Orville, there were many more honors and awards.

His friend and biographer, Fred C. Kelly, once asked Orville about his biggest "kick" in his long life as an inventor and engineer. Was it the moment that the *Flyer* actually took off in 1903?

"I got more thrill out of flying before I had ever been in the air at all—while lying in bed thinking how exciting it would be to fly," was Orville's reply.

Orville Wright suffered a heart attack on October 10, 1947. After a brief hospital stay, he returned home. He was told to slow down.

He had a second heart attack on January 27, 1948. He died three days later in a Dayton hospital. He was seventy-seven.

In his will, Orville asked that the 1903 *Flyer* be turned over to the Smithsonian Institution. Today, the first powered airplane to fly successfully hangs in the air inside the entrance to the Smithsonian's National Air and Space Museum in Washington, D.C.

It is not a model. It is not a reproduction. It is, as museum staff members stress, "the actual first airplane to fly."

Museum visitors are able to view dozens of other aircraft important in aviation history. There's the *Spirit of St. Louis*, the plane piloted in 1927 by Charles Lindbergh on the first solo flight across the Atlantic Ocean.

A silvery Douglas DC-3 that dates to 1937 is on

In his later years, Orville Wright sometimes worked on small-scale inventions, seeking to solve problems that interested him. This photograph dates to around 1947.

display. The DC-3, a twin-engine aircraft, was the first successful passenger airliner.

The rocket-powered Bell XS-1 also has a place of honor in the museum. On October 14, 1947, Captain Charles E. "Chuck" Yeager, at the controls of the XS-1, became the first pilot to fly faster than the speed of sound.

These famous aircraft and the many others on exhibit at the museum have one thing in common. They might never have come into being were it not for the first Wright *Flyer* and what the Wright brothers achieved with the aircraft.

Darrell Collins, the National Park Service historian at the Wright Brothers National Memorial in Kill Devil Hills, speaks often of that achievement. "Before the Wright brothers, no one in aviation did anything fundamentally right," he says. "Since the Wright brothers, no one has done anything fundamentally different."

CHRONOLOGY

1867   (April 16) Wilbur Wright is born near Millville, Indiana.

1871   (August 19) Orville Wright is born in Dayton, Ohio.

1893   Wright brothers open a bicycle shop in Dayton.

1899   Brothers build and test-fly a biplane kite.

1900   Wrights conduct first glider test flights at Kitty Hawk, North Carolina.

1903   Brothers fly first manned and controlled heavier-than-air machine at Kill Devil Hills, North Carolina.

1906–5 Brothers develop the first practical airplane.

1906   U.S. government grants a patent to the Wright brothers for the first flying machine.

1908   U.S. Army agrees to purchase Wright *Flyer*. The Wright Company is formed.

1911   Wilbur sets world's glider soaring record at Kill Devil Hills.

1912   (May 30) Wilbur Wright dies.

1920   Orville is appointed a member of the National Advisory Committee for Aeronautics.

1932   Wright Brothers National Memorial is dedicated at Kill Devil Hills.

1948   (January 30) Orville Wright dies.

BIBLIOGRAPHY

Primary Sources

The Papers of Wilbur and Orville Wright, Including the Chanute-Wright Letters. McFarland, Marvin W., Editor. Two Volumes. New York: McGraw-Hill, 2001.

Wright, Orville. *How We Invented the Airplane: An Illustrated History.* New York: Dover Books, 1988.

Note: For a state-by-state (or, in Canada, a province-by-province) listing of libraries, colleges, historical societies, and other institutions where primary sources are to be found, visit this Web site:

www.uidaho.edu/special-collections/east2html

Secondary Sources

Coombs, Harry and Martin Caidin. *Kill Devil Hill: Discovering the Secret of the Wright Brothers.* Boston: Houghton Mifflin, 1979.

Crouch, Tom. *The Bishop's Boys: A Life of Wilbur and Orville Wright.* New York: Norton, 1989.

Howard, Fred. *Wilbur and Orville: A Biography of the Wright Brothers.* Mineola, New York: Dover Publications, 1998.

Kelly, Fred C. *The Wright Brothers: A Biography Authorized by Orville Wright.* Boston: Little, Brown, 1943.

Walsh, John Evangelist. *One Day at Kitty Hawk: The Untold Story of the Wright Brothers and the Airplane.* New York: Crowell, 1975.

FURTHER READING

Franchere, Ruth. *The Wright Brothers*. New York: Crowell, 1972.

Freedman, Russell. *The Wright Brothers: How They Invented the Airplane*. New York: Holiday House, 1991.

Graves, Charles. *The Wright Brothers*. New York: G. P. Putnam's, 1973.

Parker, Steve. *The Wright Brothers and Aviation*. Philadelphia: Chelsea House, 1995.

Sobol, Donald. J. *The Wright Brothers at Kitty Hawk*. New York: Scholastic Paperbacks, 1961. Reissue edition 1989.

Stevenson, Augusta. *Wilbur and Orville Wright: Young Fliers*. New York: Aladdin Books, 1986.

FOR MORE INFORMATION

Wright Brothers National Memorial
Request a brochure titled "Wright Brothers National Memorial."

(National Park Service, Outer Banks Group, 1401 National Park Dr.,
Manteo, NC 27954)
Phone: (252) 441-7430
Web site: www.nps.gov/wrbr

Dayton Aviation National Historical Park
Request a packet containing descriptive information about park
historical sites.

(P. O. Box 9280, Wright Brothers Station, Dayton, OH 45409)
Phone: (837) 225-7705
Web site: www.nps.gov/daav

National Air and Space Museum
Request a booklet titled "Museum Guide."

(Smithsonian Institution, Washington, DC 29560)
Web site: www.nasm.edu

Outer Banks Chamber of Commerce
Request a booklet titled "North Carolina's Outer Banks Vacation
Guide."

(P. O. Box 1757, Kill Devil Hills, NC 27948)
Phone: (252) 441-8144
Web site: www.outerbankschamber.com

ACKNOWLEDGMENTS

Many people helped me in providing background information and photographs to be used in this book. Special thanks are due Darrell Collins, Historian, Wright Brothers National Memorial, Kill Devil Hills, NC; Joseph Hardman, First Flight Society, Kill Devil Hills, NC; Kristine L. Kaske, Archivist, National Air and Space Museum; John Sanford, Paul Lawrence Dunbar Library, Wright State University; Maja Keech, Library of Congress; and Tim Sullivan for his help and companionship at Kill Devil Hills.

George Sullivan, New York City

PHOTO CREDITS

Library of Congress (Washington, D.C.): 7, 26, 31, 35, 39, 45, 46, 52, 65, 70, 74, 79, 80, 96, 98, 107, 109; Special Collections and Archives, Paul Laurence Dunbar Library, Wright State University (Dayton, OH): 10, 15 (left), 15 (right), 17 (left), 17 (right), 52, 60, 64, 94; George Sullivan: 19, 25, 112; Smithsonian Institution, National Air and Space Museum (Washington, DC): 85, 90, 103, 115; AP/Wide World Photos: 105

INDEX

Bold numbers refer to photographs

ABOUT THE AUTHOR

George Sullivan is the author of a good-sized shelf of books for children and young adults. They cover a wide range of topics, from witchcraft to nuclear submarines, from baseball and field hockey to photography.

His interest in photography goes beyond merely writing about it. He often takes photos to illustrate his books.

His other titles for Scholastic include *Mr. President: A Book of U.S. Presidents*, *100 Years in Photographs*, and *Alamo!*

He has also written a number of biographies for the In Their Own Words series. These include *Paul Revere*, *Lewis and Clark*, *Abraham Lincoln*, *Helen Keller*, *Harriet Tubman*, *Davy Crockett*, *Thomas Edison*, and *Pocahontas*.

Mr. Sullivan was born in Lowell, Massachusetts, and brought up in Springfield, Massachusetts, where he attended public schools.

He graduated from Fordham University and worked in public relations in New York City before he began writing on a full-time basis.

Mr. Sullivan lives in New York City with his wife. He is a member of PEN, the Authors Guild, and the Society of Writers and Illustrators of Children's Books.